I0762745

Dedicated to Mom, for being my sous-chef and always staying up late with me while I bake, and Dad, for being my number-one supporter.

Thank you, Miss Julia, for teaching me tips and tricks for my treats, and thank you, Uncle Steve, for photographing all my desserts.

www.mascotbooks.com

Floating in Sweets: Delightful Desserts for Kids

Cover and spot illustrations by Tim Crecelius

All recipes have been tested and used successfully by the author, but results may vary. The author and publisher advise readers to take full responsibility for their nutrition and diet and know their restrictions. Before baking the recipes described in this book, be sure to evaluate the ingredients for any possible allergies or interactions, and do not bake beyond your level of skill or comfort level. Children should be supervised by an adult, and readers should always follow best practices for safe food preparation. The publisher and the author assume no responsibility for errors, inaccuracies, omissions, or any other inconsistencies herein. All such instances are unintentional and the author's own.

For more information, please contact:
Mascot Books, an imprint of Amplify Publishing Group
620 Herndon Parkway, Suite 220
Herndon, VA 20170
info@mascotbooks.com

Library of Congress Control Number: 2024903765
CPSIA Code: PRV1025A
ISBN-13: 979-8-89138-993-9

Printed in the United States

Ria Lala
Floating in Sweets
Delightful Desserts for Kids

Contents

I want you to close your eyes and have someone read this to you. Imagine sitting on the couch watching your favorite movie or reading your favorite book late at night and smelling warm chocolate and sugar in the oven. The cookies are taken out of the oven, and you run to the tray to get a cookie and fill up a glass of cold milk. It is warm and gooey and falls apart when you pick it up, and you finish it so fast you go back for seconds. That is the amazing sensation I want you to feel when you're making all these different types of cookies.

White Chocolate Macadamia Nut Cookies

Ingredients:

COOKIE BASE

2 sticks softened unsalted butter
½ cup granulated sugar
½ tsp vanilla extract
1 ½ cups all-purpose flour
½ tsp baking soda
½ cup white chocolate chips
½ cup dry-roasted macadamia nuts
White chocolate bar and roasted macadamias for garnishing on top

Directions:

1. Preheat the oven to 350°F and line a baking tray with parchment paper.
2. In a large bowl or stand mixer, beat the butter and sugar together until the mixture fully combines and turns soft. Then, add the vanilla extract and mix it in. After that, combine the all-purpose flour and baking soda in a separate bowl. Gradually mix it in the butter mixture until the dough is almost fully combined.
3. Add the macadamia nuts and white chocolate chips by folding them in the dough with a spatula.
4. Using an ice cream scoop, scoop the dough out of the bowl and onto the parchment paper. Press it down and make sure it has a round shape to it. Bake for 12–15 minutes or until the cookies are golden brown on the sides and the dough doesn't look wet. You're going to have to bake them in two different batches because there will be a lot of dough!
5. Have an adult help you take the cookies out of the oven. While they cool, melt your white chocolate by cutting or breaking the bar into smaller pieces and melting it in a microwave-safe bowl until there are no more chunks of chocolate. Then, put your macadamia nuts in a bag and crush them until there are both large and small pieces. Transfer them to a baking tray lined with parchment paper and roast for five minutes in the oven or until they turn slightly brown. You can use the same tray that had the cookies on them earlier!
6. Drizzle the melted chocolate over the cookies or use a spoon to pour and drench the cookies with the delicious chocolate. Sprinkle your crushed macadamia nuts on top of the cookies and enjoy!

Tip! Crush the macadamia nuts into smaller pieces if you don't want large chunks of nuts in the cookies.

The Citrus
Duo Cookies

Ingredients:

COOKIE BASE (BOTH)

2 cups all-purpose flour, plus extra for rolling the dough
2 sticks unsalted butter, room temperature
⅔ cup granulated sugar
1 ½ tsp vanilla extract
⅛ tsp salt

LEMON BASE

2 tsp fresh lemon juice
Zest of 1 lemon

ORANGE BASE

3 tsp fresh orange juice
Zest of 1 orange

GLAZE

2 cups confectioners' sugar
10 tsp milk
¼ tsp vanilla extract
Pinch of salt
Yellow and orange food coloring

Directions:

1. Preheat the oven to 325°F and put parchment paper on your baking or cookie tray.
2. In a stand mixer, beat the butter and sugar on medium speed until it combines and becomes smooth, about two minutes. Turn off the mixer and scrape the sides and bottom of the bowl so the butter–sugar mixture is mixed evenly. Turn the mixer on low and add in the vanilla extract, flour, and salt until you can squish it in your hands like soft clay (it shouldn't be sticky).
3. After that, use your spatula or your hands to split the dough in half. Add the lemon juice and zest to one half of the dough, and mix until combined. Repeat the process with the other half, adding the orange juice and zest, then mixing until combined.
4. Cover each dough separately in plastic wrap and put in the fridge for 10 minutes or the freezer for 5 minutes.
5. Take the lemon cookie dough out of the fridge and put it on a giant flour-coated cutting board or flat surface with flour (keep the orange cookie dough in the fridge so it stays cool). Cover the dough with flour too, and with a rolling pin, roll your dough and cut out cookies with the lemon-shaped cookie cutter.
6. Put them on the parchment-paper-lined tray and bake for 12 minutes or until they turn a light golden-brown color. While that batch is baking, take your orange-flavored cookie dough out of the fridge and repeat the rolling and cutting process. Make sure an adult helps you take the cookies out of the oven and put the next ones in the oven.
7. While the cookies are cooling, start the glaze. In a small bowl, whisk all the glaze ingredients until they come together. Then split the glaze into two bowls and dye one with yellow food coloring for the lemon cookies and the other with orange food coloring for the orange cookies. Put each color of glaze in its own plastic bag (with a very small hole cut in the corner) or piping bag (I like the piping bag better). Pipe the outline of the cookie (that means just around the outer edge of the cookie).
8. Once you have done that to all the cookies, pour the icing into separate bowls and add one more teaspoon of milk to both glazes to thin them out. Pour the icing back into the bags. Then, pipe a dollop of the icing in the center of the cookie and spread it out to the edges with a flatter knife. Don't overfill the center or else it will spill out! You can always add more if you don't have enough! The glaze takes a day to set, but you can always just eat the cookie right after! Enjoy!

Pumpkin Spice
Cookies

Ingredients:

COOKIE BASE

1 ½ sticks unsalted butter, room temperature
½ cup canned pure pumpkin puree
½ cup light brown sugar
1 tsp vanilla extract
2 cups flour
1 tsp pumpkin pie spice
½ tsp baking soda

CREAM CHEESE ICING

4 Tbsp block cream cheese
2 Tbsp confectioners' sugar
½ tsp vanilla extract
1 Tbsp milk

Directions:

1. Preheat the oven to 350°F and line a baking tray with parchment paper.
2. Beat the butter, pumpkin puree, and light brown sugar in a large bowl or stand mixer until combined. Then, add the vanilla extract and mix again. Add the flour, baking soda, and pumpkin pie spice to the wet ingredients and beat until it forms a cookie-dough consistency.
3. Roll into balls or roll on a flat surface and cut with a cookie cutter. Bake for 12 minutes or until the cookie turns a slightly darker shade of brown on the sides. Have an adult help you take them out of the oven and let them cool.
4. Meanwhile, make the icing. Combine all the icing ingredients in a small bowl and mix until smooth. You can either pipe or spread onto the cookies. Sprinkle with a little ground cinnamon or pumpkin pie spice on top of the cookies and enjoy!

Honey Snickerpoodle
Cookies

Ingredients:

COOKIE BASE

2 sticks unsalted butter
¼ cup light brown sugar
¼ cup honey
1 tsp vanilla extract
2 cups all-purpose flour
½ tsp baking soda
1 ½ tsp cornstarch
Candy eyes, lips, accessories, etc. (these are found in cake stores and online too!)

CINNAMON-SUGAR COATING

½ cup granulated sugar
1 Tbsp ground cinnamon

HONEY BUTTER

¼ cup softened butter
2 Tbsp honey

Directions:

1. Preheat the oven to 350°F and line a baking tray with parchment paper.
2. Get a big bowl and whisk the soft butter, sugar, and honey until the ingredients are combined and smooth. Then, add the vanilla extract and mix. After, add the all-purpose flour, baking soda, and cornstarch and mix until you have a moldable dough.
3. Roll out your dough and cut with a dog-head-shaped cookie cutter. Put the dog-shaped cookie dough cutouts in the fridge for 10 minutes.
4. After, make the coating by mixing the sugar and cinnamon in a small bowl with a spoon. Then, coat the cookies in the cinnamon sugar (make sure to cover all sides).
5. Place on the parchment paper and bake for 12 minutes (don't bake much longer than this—the chewier the better!).
6. Have an adult help you take the cookies out of the oven and let them cool.
7. Make the honey butter by combining the soft butter and honey until smooth and light. Use this honey butter as "glue" to stick the candy eyes and accessories on the dog cookies. Decorate it any way you like. Go crazy and enjoy!

Raspberry
Heart Cookies

Ingredients:

COOKIE BASE

2 sticks softened unsalted butter
¾ cup granulated sugar
1 tsp vanilla extract
Pinch of salt
2 cups all-purpose flour
½ tsp baking soda
8 tsp raspberry puree, strained (puree a whole box of raspberries and keep the rest for the glaze)

RASPBERRY GLAZE

Leftover raspberry puree
2 cups confectioners' sugar

Directions:

1. Line a baking tray with parchment paper and preheat the oven to 350°F.
2. Combine the butter, sugar, vanilla, salt, and raspberry puree in a bowl and mix until smooth. Then, add the flour and baking soda and mix until a dough forms.
3. Roll out the dough and cut into heart shapes of all sizes.
4. Have an adult help you place cookies on the baking tray and bake for 10 minutes or until the sides have browned slightly.
5. While they're in the oven, make the glaze. Take the leftover puree and confectioners' sugar and put them in a bowl. Mix with a small whisk or spoon until it reaches a thicker glaze-like consistency.
6. Once the cookies are done, decorate them with the glaze any way you like. After putting the glaze on the cookies, make sure to let them sit for a few minutes so the glaze design doesn't get messed up (if the glaze is still wet on the cookie, it can smudge if moved around immediately). You can make polka dots or stripes by carefully drawing lines and dots all over the cookies, or you can come up with your own cool designs. Grab your favorite designed cookie and enjoy!

Cupcakes

I want you to close your eyes and have someone read this to you. Imagine walking into a bakery that is super colorful. You hear the machines whirling. You walk up to the cupcake display case and see all the different colors and piping designs of the frosting. The cake decorator tells you all the different flavors—and her favorites. You choose to take a dozen cupcakes of all different flavors because you can't decide which ones you want to eat. That is the feeling I want you to get when you are making all these different-flavored cupcakes.

S'mores Sticky Situation Cupcakes

Ingredients:

CUPCAKES (GROUP 1)

1 ¼ cups all-purpose flour
½ tsp baking soda
½ tsp salt
¾ cup milk
½ cup unsweetened cocoa powder

CUPCAKES (GROUP 2)

1 cup granulated sugar
¾ cup vegetable oil
¼ cup applesauce
1 tsp vanilla extract
½ cup semisweet chocolate chips

FROSTING

1 ½ sticks unsalted butter, soft but not melted (put in the microwave for 20–25 seconds if straight out of the refrigerator)
2 cups confectioners' sugar
Pinch of salt
1 ½ tsp vanilla extract
2 Tbsp honey
1 Tbsp milk

FILLING/TOPPINGS

1 vegan mini marshmallow for the filling (inside of each baked cupcake)
Crushed graham crackers and 1 burnt/golden marshmallow on top

Directions:

CUPCAKES

1. Set the oven to convection and 350°F.
2. Get a cupcake tin and line each cup with liners.
3. Now start on making the cupcake batter. Add the all-purpose flour, baking soda, and salt in the group 1 ingredients to a small bowl and whisk. Set the bowl to the side and get your small saucepan.
4. In a saucepan on the stove, heat the milk until small bubbles form on the sides of the saucepan, then turn off the heat. Make sure an adult helps you with the stove!
5. Put your unsweetened cocoa powder in a large bowl. Pour the hot milk on the powder and mix until it looks like chocolate milk. Then, add all the group 2 ingredients to the cocoa mixture EXCEPT the chocolate chips. Whisk everything together until combined. The oil will stay on top of everything else.
6. Mix the remaining group 1 ingredients (the ones in step 3) with the group 2 mixture until it looks like a yummy chocolate cake batter. Fold in the chocolate chips. With an ice cream scoop, pour the batter in the liners and bake for 20 minutes or until you can stick a toothpick in and it comes out clean.

FROSTING

1. Combine the butter with a handheld or stand mixer until it becomes soft and fluffy (the butter should be soft when whipping it).
2. Add the sugar and salt, then mix. Now add the vanilla extract and honey and combine until smooth. Finally, add the milk and mix until fluffy!
3. Put frosting into a piping bag with your favorite tip and set it aside.
4. Take a mini marshmallow and use a firepit or your gas stovetop and roast your marshmallow to your desired liking! Insert it into the cupcakes by making a hole or pushing the marshmallow into the center of the cupcake.
5. Then, frost the cupcakes. Make sure they aren't steaming hot when you put the frosting on or the cake will melt the frosting. Carefully swirl the frosting around the top of the cupcake, going from the outside and swirling it in to the middle.
6. Sprinkle your crushed graham crackers and place another marshmallow (golden or burnt) on the top of your cupcakes. Serve them and enjoy!

Roses-Are-Red Velvet Cupcakes

Ingredients:

CUPCAKES (GROUP 1)

1 ½ cups all-purpose flour
2 Tbsp unsweetened cocoa powder
½ tsp baking soda
¼ tsp salt

CUPCAKES (GROUP 2)

½ cup vegetable oil
½ cup buttermilk
¼ cup unsweetened applesauce
¾ cup granulated sugar
1 tablespoon distilled white vinegar
1 ¼ tsp vanilla extract
½ cup white chocolate chips
Few drops of red food coloring

FROSTING

1 ½ sticks unsalted butter
2 cups confectioners' sugar
Pinch of salt
1 tsp vanilla extract
1 tsp rose water
Few drops of pink food coloring

Tip! Cupcake batter consistency should look smooth and luscious. Sometimes it will be thick and sometimes thin, but there should be no lumps and spots of unmixed ingredients.

Directions:

CUPCAKES

1. Set the oven to 350°F and place cupcake liners in your cupcake tray.
2. Combine the group 1 ingredients in a small bowl.
3. In a larger bowl, add the group 2 ingredients (EXCEPT THE WHITE CHOCOLATE CHIPS) and whisk together to combine. Then, add the group 1 mixture to the group 2 mixture and whisk until smooth. Lastly, fold in the white chocolate chips.
4. With an ice cream scoop, scoop the batter into the liners. Bake for 20 minutes, or until you can stick a toothpick in and it comes out clean with no batter or cake crumbles on it. Take the cupcakes out of the oven and let them cool.

FROSTING

1. Beat the butter, sugar, and salt until the ingredients combine into a paste-like mixture. Then, add the vanilla extract and rose water until perfectly smooth.
2. Use the tip of a toothpick by dipping it in the pink food coloring and swirling a very small amount into the frosting to give a faint pink color. (Keep the leftover frosting and dye it green. Then use it to make the leaves—but the leaves are optional and just add a little flair! It will look like these beautiful cupcakes are in an enchanted garden!)
3. Transfer the pink frosting to a piping bag and pipe beautiful roses with the frosting. To do this, start by piping in the middle of the cupcake and keep swirling out until you get to the edge of the cupcake base. Add the optional green leaves by piping the little green frosting on the side of the roses and enjoy!

Churro Cupcakes

Ingredients:

CUPCAKES (GROUP 1)

1¼ cups all-purpose flour
1 tsp baking powder
½ tsp salt
1 tsp ground cinnamon

CUPCAKES (GROUP 2)

1 stick unsalted butter
¾ cup granulated sugar
½ cup applesauce
1 ½ tsp vanilla extract
½ cup milk

CARAMEL

¼ cup light brown sugar
¾ cup granulated sugar
7 Tbsp salted butter, cold
½ cup heavy cream
½ tsp vanilla extract
1 tsp pink Himalayan salt

FROSTING

1 ½ sticks unsalted butter
2 cups confectioners' sugar
Pinch of salt
1 tsp vanilla extract
3 tsp homemade caramel (more if needed for tan color)

CHURRO BITES

Go to your local bakery or the grocery store and buy churro bites that are mini!
Use leftover caramel* to top cupcakes and to dip leftover churro bites

Directions:

1. Preheat your oven to 350°F and line your cupcake tins with colorful liners.
2. Combine the group 1 ingredients in a medium-sized bowl and mix.
3. In a larger bowl, combine the butter and sugar together with a handheld or stand mixer until it is smooth and creamy. After that, slowly add in the applesauce and vanilla extract until it combines (it may look a little unusual, but that is OK!).
4. While continuing to mix the group 2 ingredients in the large bowl, pour a small amount of the group 1 ingredient mixture into the group 2 ingredient mixture until they combine. Then, pour a small amount of milk and combine. Alternate these until all the group 1 ingredient mixture and milk have been incorporated.
5. Pour the cinnamon cupcake batter into your cupcake tins and bake for about 20 minutes, or until your wooden toothpick has no batter on it after inserting it into a cupcake.
6. While the cupcakes are baking, make the caramel. Melt down both the brown and granulated sugars in a medium saucepan until they have completely melted. Now, add the butter. Once the cold butter melts, immediately add the heavy cream and stir until everything comes together. Let the mixture boil, and then stir in the vanilla extract and salt. Take it off the heat and strain it into another bowl so there are no chunks of sugar that didn't melt left over in your caramel.
7. While the caramel and cupcakes cool, make the frosting. Mix the soft butter with a handheld or stand mixer until it is smooth. Then, add the sugar and salt. Once that's combined, add the vanilla extract.
8. Once the caramel is cool, mix it into the frosting until it has a subtle tan color. It will give it a nice light caramel flavor (a stronger caramel flavor will come out in the drizzle topping).
9. Decorate your cupcakes with the frosting and caramel drizzle and place the churro bites on top (you can buy mini churro bites or make mini ones at home!). Enjoy!

*The picture shows a melted chocolate drizzle instead of caramel. Both taste delicious on these cupcakes so you can decide which drizzle you would like to put on top!

Neapolitan-Pop Cupcakes

Ingredients:

CUPCAKES (GROUP 1)

1 ¼ cups all-purpose flour
1 tsp baking powder
¼ tsp salt

BUTTER AND SUGAR MIXTURE

1 stick unsalted butter
¾ cup granulated sugar

CUPCAKES (GROUP 2)

½ cup applesauce
½ tsp vanilla extract
1 vanilla bean (you're adding the scraped seeds)
½ cup milk

STRAWBERRY FILLING

1 cup strawberries (cut in quarters)
¼ cup granulated sugar
1 tsp cornstarch
2 tsp fresh lemon juice
¼ cup water

CHOCOLATE FROSTING

1 stick unsalted butter
2 cups confectioners' sugar
½ cup melted semisweet chocolate
1 ½ Tbsp unsweetened cocoa powder
3 Tbsp milk
½ tsp vanilla extract

TOPPING

Crushed Oreos!

Directions:

1. Set your oven to 350°F and place cupcake liners in your cupcake tins.
2. In a medium-sized bowl, mix the group 1 ingredients until combined.
3. In a separate bowl, beat the butter and sugar mixture together with a handheld or stand mixer until it looks creamy and fully mixed together.
4. Add the group 2 ingredients (EXCEPT THE MILK) to the butter mixture until fully mixed.
5. In the same bowl, alternate the group 1 ingredients and milk (about half the mixture at a time, starting and ending with group 1 ingredients) until you've used it all.
6. Scoop the batter into the cupcake tin and bake for around 18–20 minutes. Take it out when the toothpick does not have any cake batter marks on it. (Let an adult help you with that!)
7. Make the filling. Add the filling ingredients group into a saucepan and stir until the mixture starts bubbling (like a witch's cauldron!) and then turn off the heat. Make sure you don't burn it! You will know when it is done when the strawberries are soft enough that if you were to squish them with a spoon, the spoon would press down easily (and the mixture is bubbling all throughout).
8. Make the frosting. Combine the frosting ingredients group in a food processor until it is fully smooth and all one color of chocolate brown.
9. Fill the cupcakes by scooping out the middle of the cupcake and adding a spoonful of the strawberry filling. Then, put the cake bits you removed back on top. Frost the cupcakes, sprinkle with Oreos, and enjoy!

Triple Berry Cupcakes

Ingredients:

CUPCAKES (GROUP 1)

1 ⅓ cups all-purpose flour

1 tsp baking powder

¼ tsp salt

CUPCAKES (GROUP 2)

1 stick softened unsalted butter

¾ cup granulated sugar

½ cup unsweetened applesauce

1 tsp vanilla extract

¼ cup strained strawberry puree

¼ cup milk

RASPBERRY "SOAK"/DRIZZLE

1 box fresh raspberries

1 tsp lemon zest

1 tsp lemon juice

1 tsp cornstarch

¼ cup water

BLUEBERRY FROSTING

1 ½ sticks unsalted butter

2 cups confectioners' sugar

1 tsp vanilla extract

Pinch of salt

1 tsp milk

2 Tbsp blended frozen blueberries

Directions:

1. Preheat the oven to 350°F and put cupcake liners in your cupcake tin.
2. Whisk the group 1 ingredients together in a medium-sized bowl.
3. In a separate bowl, combine the butter and sugar with a stand or handheld mixer until it is soft and grainy. Then, add the applesauce and vanilla extract and mix until combined.
4. Put a scoop of the group 1 ingredients mixture into the bowl, and when fully combined, add the strawberry puree into the batter and mix.
5. Add another scoop of the group 1 ingredients mixture, then add the milk and mix until all ingredients are fully incorporated together.
6. Add the rest of the group 1 ingredients mixture and mix until the cupcake batter is smooth and luscious.
7. Pour cupcake batter in the tins and bake for 20 minutes or until a toothpick comes out clean.

RASPBERRY "SOAK"/DRIZZLE

1. Combine all the ingredients in a small saucepan until the mixture bubbles. Once bubbling, turn off the heat.
2. Strain the mixture to remove the seeds. Let it cool. (This is to give a sour surprise in the middle of the cupcake—it is supposed to be a gooey liquid.)

BLUEBERRY FROSTING

1. Using a handheld or stand mixer, beat the butter until smooth. Add sugar and salt and mix together.
2. Add vanilla extract and mix until creamy.
3. Add milk and blended frozen blueberries until the mixture is smooth and has a nice bluish/purple color.
4. Once cupcakes are cool, use a syringe or squeeze bottle to poke a hole in the cupcake and inject the raspberry drizzle. Top the cupcakes with your delicious frosting, piped or spread, and enjoy!

Twincesses Duo Cupcakes

Lemon Rose

Lemon Rose Cupcake Ingredients:

CUPCAKES (GROUP 1)

1 ⅓ cups all-purpose flour
1 tsp baking powder
½ tsp salt
1 stick softened unsalted butter
¾ cup granulated sugar

CUPCAKES (GROUP 2)

¼ cup applesauce
1 ½ tsp vanilla extract
1 medium lemon's worth of lemon zest
1 tsp lemon juice
½ cup milk

BUTTERCREAM FILLING

5 Tbsp super-soft unsalted butter
3 ½ Tbsp confectioners' sugar
¼ tsp vanilla bean paste
2 tsp milk

ROSE FROSTING

1 ½ sticks unsalted butter
2 cups confectioners' sugar
½ tsp vanilla extract
1 tsp rose water
1 Tbsp milk
1 drop pink food coloring

Lemon Rose Cupcake Directions:

1. Line a cupcake tin with cupcake liners and preheat the oven to 350°F.
2. Combine the group 1 ingredients (EXCEPT the butter and sugar) and mix.
3. Beat the butter and sugar together until the mixture is soft and grainy. Turn the mixer on low and add the group 2 ingredients (EXCEPT the milk) to the same bowl until all the ingredients are fully mixed in.
4. Add half the group 1 ingredient mixture into the group 2 ingredient mixture. Now add all the milk and then the rest of the group 1 ingredient mixture. Turn it up to medium speed and mix until all the ingredients are combined.
5. Scoop the batter into the cupcake tins and bake this set of cupcakes for 20 minutes or until the toothpick comes out clean.
6. Now, prepare the buttercream filling by mixing (with a spatula) the softened butter and when smooth, add the confectioners' sugar, one tablespoon at a time. Then, add in the vanilla bean paste and mix until fully combined. Put it in a piping bag if you want to pipe it into the cupcakes. Or you could keep it in the bowl and spoon it in. Set the filling aside for now.
7. Make the frosting by combining the butter and sugar first and then the rest of the rose frosting ingredients.
8. Assemble the cupcakes by scooping out the middle of the cupcakes and adding the buttercream filling. Then, fill the hole with the cake you took out and pipe the luscious rose frosting on top. Now, you will have Topaz's sixteenth-birthday-inspired cupcakes.

These cupcakes were inspired by the novel *Twincesses*, written by my older sister, Tara Lala. In the book, the twin sisters, Topaz and Lotus, each have a sixteenth-birthday cake made especially for them. These are the cupcake versions of the sisters' birthday cakes.

Twincesses
TARA LALA
Twincesses Duo Cupcakes
Chocolate
Blueberry

Chocolate Blueberry Cupcake Ingredients:

CUPCAKES (GROUP 1)

1 ¼ cups all-purpose flour
½ tsp baking soda
½ tsp salt
¾ cup unsweetened cocoa powder
1 cup milk, heated

CUPCAKES (GROUP 2)

½ cup light brown sugar
½ cup granulated sugar
¾ cup vegetable oil
¼ cup applesauce
1 tsp vanilla extract

CHOCOLATE FILLING

1 cup semisweet chocolate chips
¾ cup heavy cream (heated)

BLUEBERRY FROSTING

1 ½ sticks unsalted butter
2 cups confectioners' sugar
½ tsp vanilla extract
2 Tbsp + 1 tsp fresh blueberries (blended)
Blue food dye

Chocolate Blueberry Cupcake Directions:

1. Preheat the oven to 350°F and line a cupcake tin with cupcake liners.
2. Add the group 1 ingredients (EXCEPT the unsweetened cocoa powder and milk) to a medium-sized bowl and mix.
3. Put the already-heated milk and cocoa powder into a large bowl and mix until smooth. It will smell like very delicious hot chocolate.
4. Mix the group 2 ingredients into the cocoa powder mixture until smooth. The oil will sit on top of the ingredients, but that is supposed to happen!
5. Add the group 1 ingredient mixture to the group 2 mixture and whisk until smooth. Pour the batter into the cupcake tins. Bake for 20 minutes or until a toothpick comes out clean.
6. Make the chocolate filling. Heat the heavy cream on the stove, and just as it comes to a boil, add it to the measured-out chocolate and mix until the mixture is all combined and gets a little bit thicker (it will thicken more as it cools). If all the chocolate chips don't melt when mixed with the hot heavy cream, add the mixture back to the saucepan that you boiled your heavy cream in and mix until all the chocolate chips are melted. Now let it cool.
7. While it is cooling, make the frosting by combining the butter and sugar with a handheld or stand mixer until it looks soft and not clumpy.
8. Add the vanilla extract and blueberries until the mixture is smooth and has a nice color to it. Add a couple drops of blue food dye if you want the bluish-purple color in your frosting, but if you don't want to add the food dye, the natural color is pretty too (just not as blue).
9. Assemble the cupcakes. Poke a hole in the middle of a cupcake—you can use a spoon or something that will make a medium-sized hole in the cupcake—and fill it with your cooled ganache. (Make sure to put the cake you took out back on top of the filling to cover it.) Pipe your luscious frosting on top, and you will have Lotus's sixteenth-birthday-inspired cupcakes.

TAILS
FROM DOWNUNDER

Cheesecakes

I want you to close your eyes and have someone read this to you. Have you ever walked into an ice cream store and smelled the buttery waffle cones and the sugary, cold ice cream? Well, that's the exact scent you will smell when these cheesecakes are baking in the oven. They take a long time to bake, so make sure you are watching your favorite TV show or movie while waiting. The smell fills the kitchen and the entire home.

Banana Cream
Pie Cheesecake

Ingredients:

NILLA WAFER CRUST

1 ½ cups Nilla Wafers
4 Tbsp melted unsalted butter
½ cup pecan pieces

VANILLA CHEESECAKE BATTER

3 blocks cream cheese
¼ cup granulated sugar
½ tsp vanilla extract
1 ½ tsp vanilla pudding powder
¼ cup Just Egg (this is a liquid egg substitute!)
3 Tbsp milk

TOPPINGS

Whipped cream
Sliced bananas
Crushed pecan pieces

Directions:

1. Preheat the oven to 350°F and cut out a circle of parchment paper to put on the bottom of the cheesecake pan so the crust doesn't stick to it. Spray the paper with a nonstick baking spray that has flour in it. If you want, you can also spray some between the pan and the parchment paper so the paper will stay on the pan.
2. Pulse the crust ingredients in the food processor until it is moldable/comes together. Make sure it does not feel dry and powdery. Spoon the crust into the sprayed cheesecake pan and press it down to evenly smoothe out the crust over the whole bottom of the pan. Now, start on the cheesecake batter.
3. Combine all the batter ingredients with a handheld or stand mixer until smooth. Then pour the batter over the crust in the pan and bake for about an hour. You'll know the cheesecake is done when it has brown spots or a slight brown color on top. You may need to bake it for an extra 15 minutes; it just depends on your oven.
4. Have an adult help you take it out of the oven, and let it cool in the fridge until it is completely cold (I recommend keeping it in there overnight so the runny batter in the middle firms up). When your cheesecake is cooled completely, remove it from the pan and carefully take the parchment paper off the bottom of the crust. Decorate it with whipped cream (in the photo, I made rosette flowers by making swirls just like the frosting in the Roses-Are-Red Velvet Cupcake recipe). Place sliced bananas on top of each rosette and sprinkle with crushed pecans. Enjoy!

Strawberry Lemonade
Cheesecake

Ingredients:

LEMON GRAHAM CRACKER CRUST

DRY CRUST INGREDIENTS

9 graham crackers
3 Tbsp granulated sugar
1 tsp lemon zest

WET CRUST INGREDIENTS

1 tsp lemon juice
3 Tbsp unsalted butter

LEMON CHEESECAKE BATTER

3 blocks cream cheese
½ cup granulated sugar
1 tsp vanilla extract
1 tsp lemon zest
1 tsp lemon juice
¼ cup Just Egg

STRAWBERRY TOPPING

2 cups strawberries, cut into quarters
½ cup frozen concentrate lemonade
1 tsp cornstarch

Directions:

1. Preheat the oven to 350°F.
2. Pulse dry crust ingredients until powdery, and then add wet crust ingredients until it comes together to that moldable consistency. Then, scoop it out of the food processor and press it in a cheesecake pan that you have already lined with parchment paper and nonstick spray.
3. Make the cheesecake: Beat all the batter ingredients together until fully mixed and smooth. Pour batter into the pan with the crust already in it.
4. Bake it for about an hour or until the top is light brown in color.
5. Now, make the strawberry topping: Combine all the strawberry topping ingredients in a medium saucepan on medium heat until it bubbles. Take the mixture off the heat and let it slightly cool before putting it on the cheesecake.
6. Once the cheesecake is out of the oven, put the cooled strawberry mixture on top of the cheesecake and let the cheesecake cool completely in the fridge. (Make sure to pour the strawberry mixture on the cheesecake 5 minutes after you take the cheesecake out of the oven, and then stick it in the fridge immediately so it can cool on the cheesecake at the same time as the rest of the dessert.) Enjoy!

Tip! Put your cheesecake pan on a tray so if any butter/oil spills out, it won't go all over your oven.

Chocolate Peanut Butter Cheesecake

Ingredients:

CHOCOLATE PEANUT GRAHAM CRUST

1 cup chocolate Teddy Grahams
½ cup salted peanuts
3 Tbsp light brown sugar
4 Tbsp melted unsalted butter

PEANUT BUTTER CHEESECAKE BATTER

3 blocks cream cheese
½ cup granulated sugar
½ tsp vanilla extract
2 Tbsp creamy peanut butter
¼ cup Just Egg

CHOCOLATE WHIPPED CREAM

1 cup heavy cream
⅓ cup confectioners' sugar
½ tsp vanilla extract
⅓ cup melted chocolate chips

TOPPING

Mini Reese's Peanut Butter Cups

Directions:

1. Preheat the oven to 350°F and line your cheesecake pan with parchment paper and nonstick cooking spray that has all-purpose flour in it.
2. Using a food processor, pulse all the crust ingredients (EXCEPT THE BUTTER) until fully smooth. Then, add the butter and pulse until it all comes together. Spoon the crust into the pan and press it down evenly all over the bottom.
3. Make the cheesecake: Mix all the batter ingredients with a handheld or stand mixer until smooth. Spoon it into the cheesecake pan with the crust already in it and bake for around an hour. You may need an extra 15 minutes if the batter is still runny when the pan moves. Take the cheesecake out of the oven and stick it into the refrigerator. It should be mostly firm before it goes in the fridge, but if still a little jiggly, that is ok because the cheesecake will firm up more in the fridge.
4. Make the whipped cream: Whip all the cream group ingredients with a handheld whisk or stand mixer with a whisk attachment. Once it becomes scoopable and not runny, this will probably take 6 minutes on medium speed, pipe the whipped cream any way you like onto your fully cooled cheesecake. Pour the mini Reese's all throughout the middle of the cheesecake! Enjoy!

Tails from Down Under Cheesecake

Ingredients:

PRETZEL GRAHAM CRACKER CRUST

1 ½ cups graham cracker crumbs
½ cup crushed pretzel pieces
4 Tbsp light brown sugar
6 Tbsp melted unsalted butter

WHITE CHOCOLATE CHEESECAKE BATTER

3 blocks cream cheese
¼ cup granulated sugar
½ cup melted white chocolate
¼ cup Just Egg
1 tsp vanilla extract
Blue food dye for swirling
¼ cup heavy cream

WHITE CHOCOLATE WHIPPED CREAM

1 ½ cups heavy cream
½ cup confectioners' sugar
¼ tsp salt
½ tsp vanilla extract
½ cup white chocolate (plus extra if you want to do the optional sea creatures as a topping for the ocean-looking whipped cream!)

Directions:

1. Preheat your oven to 350°F and line your cheesecake pan with parchment paper and nonstick baking spray that has flour in the spray.
2. Make the crust: Combine the pretzel graham cracker crust ingredients (WITHOUT THE BUTTER) with a wooden spoon and then add your melted butter and mix. Press the mixture into the cheesecake pan.
3. Combine all the cheesecake batter ingredients except for the food dye. Once everything is smooth, add food coloring to half the batter and then alternate the colors as you spoon it into the cheesecake pan. (I used an ice cream scoop to alternate between the white and blue colored batters throughout the pan until all the batter was gone.) Use a toothpick to swirl the batter in the pan, making figure eights or zigzags to swirl the colors.
4. Bake it for an hour and let it cool completely in the fridge.
5. While the cheesecake cools, whisk together all of the whipped cream ingredients using a handheld or stand mixer (let the machine run as you add the ingredients one by one) until the cream is scoopable and ready to pipe.
6. Once cooled, top the cheesecake with whipped cream and pipe or spread it on the cheesecake to look like waves.
7. If you want to add little white chocolate sea creatures to the ocean on top of your cheesecake, then do this step. Melt your white chocolate. Pour the melted chocolate in sea creature molds and put the molds into the freezer for 10–15 minutes to cool. Once hard, pop them out of the pans and put fun edible glitter colors over them to make them sparkly. Place them anywhere on top of the cheesecake, and enjoy!

This cheesecake is inspired by my older sister's second book, *Tails from Down Under*, a fun deep-sea adventure in which a regular teenage girl discovers her true identity. I made the cake relating to the ocean and the wonders of the underwater world, just like how Paradise finds her own underwater world.

Piña Colada
Cheesecake

Ingredients:

COCONUT CRUST

9 graham crackers
½ cup unsweetened coconut shreds
2 Tbsp light brown sugar
4 Tbsp melted unsalted butter

PINEAPPLE CHEESECAKE BATTER

3 blocks cream cheese
½ cup granulated sugar
¼ tsp vanilla extract
¼ cup Just Egg
½ cup strained crushed pineapple (canned)

CHERRY WHIPPED CREAM

1 cup heavy cream
⅓ cup confectioners' sugar
¼ tsp vanilla extract
3 ½ tsp maraschino cherry liquid

TOPPING

Maraschino cherries

Directions:

1. Preheat the oven to 350°F. Combine the coconut crust ingredients (MINUS THE BUTTER) in a food processor until all combined and powdery. Then, add in the melted butter until it forms a crust.
2. Cut out a circle of parchment paper to fit the size of your cheesecake pan and place it on the bottom. Spray the pan with nonstick cooking spray that has flour in the spray.
3. Spoon the crust into the pan, press it down, and set aside.
4. Combine all the batter ingredients until smooth and creamy; pour all of it into the pan and bake for around an hour (you will know when it's done when there are brown bubbles on top and it has a faint tan color).
5. Let it cool in the fridge overnight so it can set. When it's all set, make the whipped cream. Combine all the ingredients in the cherry whipped cream section (while letting the machine run as you add the ingredients one by one) and let it whip until it becomes scoopable. Make sure to not overmix it! (Immediately stop mixing it when it reaches a thick consistency.) Pipe swirls on top, add your cherries onto each swirl, and enjoy!

I want you to close your eyes and have someone read this to you. Imagine a plain cake in front of you. Choose which type of frosting you want to put on it . . . chocolate, vanilla, raspberry? Now start piping the cake with this frosting, and imagine yourself decorating the cake with your favorite candies and chocolates and place them all over it. Add your final touches of edible glitter and decorations. Now think to yourself and tell me, who would you give this beautifully decorated and delicious cake to?

Strawberry
Peach Cake

Ingredients:

CAKE

2 cups cake flour
1 ½ cups granulated sugar
2 tsp baking powder
½ tsp salt
2 sticks butter
1 tsp vanilla extract
1 vanilla bean (use seeds only)
¼ cup Just Egg
1 cup buttermilk

CHEESECAKE PUDDING CUSTARD

Cheesecake-flavored pudding mix (make it according to the package)
Milk is required for the pudding mix, so use the amount that is stated
Washed fruit for topping and filling—peaches, strawberries, etc. (any fresh fruit you like)

FROSTING

1 ½ sticks unsalted butter
2 cups confectioners' sugar
½ tsp vanilla extract
1 vanilla bean (scraped seeds)
1 ½ Tbsp milk
Rainbow food coloring

Directions:

1. Preheat the oven to 350°F and then combine the dry ingredients for the cake batter: add the cake flour, sugar, baking powder, and salt into a medium-sized bowl and mix it together until the ingredients are all combined.
2. In a separate bowl, mix the butter, vanilla extract, and vanilla bean with a handheld or stand mixer until smooth. Add the rest of the batter ingredients (Just Egg and buttermilk) to the butter mixture until the batter is wet and all combined.
3. Combine both mixtures, pouring the dry into the wet until it forms a cake batter consistency. Now, prep the pans just like it tells you to do in the next step.
4. Add the cake batter to the two 8" pans coated with cooking spray with flour and lined with parchment paper and bake for 25–30 minutes.
5. Now, make the filling: Make the cheesecake pudding custard according to the package instructions and mix until it becomes thick. Put it in the refrigerator until you need to use it (this helps make the filling thicker and cold).
6. When the cake is done baking, let it cool. Then start the frosting: whip the butter with a handheld or stand mixer until it's fluffy.
7. Add the sugar and mix until combined; now, add the rest of the frosting ingredients until it is a perfect, fluffy frosting. Add the ingredients while the mixer is still running.
8. Now, assemble the cake: Pipe a ring of frosting around the outside rim of the first layer of cake. Add the cheesecake pudding filling in the middle of the ring of frosting (the center of the cake) and fill it up until it becomes leveled with the frosting ring (you may not need all of it). Then, put your favorite sliced fruit on top of the pudding. Now, put the next cake on top of that and frost the outside with the remaining frosting. Make sure to not overfill the inside or it will spill out when you put the next layer on top of this one.
9. Now, create the mermaid tail design! Make a column of dots on the crumb-coat layer of frosting and take an offset spatula and swipe it across the cake horizontally. Wherever the cake's color is faded or faint from the swipe, put another column of dots and do the same thing until you cover the whole cake. Finish decorating it like the picture, with the mermaid tail design on the side and the fruit on top, and enjoy!

Chocolate Mint Cake

Ingredients:

CAKE (GROUP 1)

¾ cup unsweetened cocoa powder
1 cup milk, hot

CAKE (GROUP 2)

1 ½ tsp baking soda
½ tsp salt
2 cups all-purpose flour
1 cup chocolate chips, plus extra for the top and middle of the cake

CAKE (GROUP 3)

1 ¼ cup granulated sugar
1 cup oil
1 ½ tsp vanilla extract
¼ cup Just Egg

FROSTING

2 ½ sticks unsalted butter
3 cups powdered sugar
⅛ tsp salt
1 tsp vanilla extract
½ tsp peppermint extract
1 Tbsp milk
Green food coloring (just a very small amount)

Directions:

1. Preheat the oven to 350°F, then start on the cake batter: Mix together the group 1 ingredients in a large bowl. When it is smooth, add all the group 3 ingredients, starting with the granulated sugar, into that same bowl and whisk until combined.
2. Add all the group 2 ingredients (EXCEPT THE CHOCOLATE CHIPS), starting with the baking soda, to the rest of the batter and mix until it forms a smooth batter. Now, add the chocolate chips and fold them in with a spatula. After the batter is done, make sure to prep the cake pans like it says below.
3. Scoop the batter into two 8″ pans that you previously sprayed with cooking spray and lined with parchment paper. Bake them for 30–35 minutes or until the toothpick comes out clean. Take the cakes out of the oven and let them cool.
4. While they're cooling, make the frosting: Mix the softened butter until it becomes soft and fluffy. Once fluffy, add the sugar and the salt until it is completely mixed together. Then, add all the other frosting ingredients and keep mixing until the frosting is super fluffy and not heavy (the longer you mix it for, the fluffier and less dense it becomes). Make sure the amount of food coloring added is a really tiny amount to get that faint mint color.
5. Stack the cakes with a layer of buttercream in the middle; sprinkle chocolate chips throughout the layer and then put the other cake on top. Now, frost the top of the cake, add a frosting border to the bottom, and add more chocolate chips on top and enjoy!

Tip! An eggless cake needs to be cooled very precisely or it will stick to the pan and not come out right. After the cake bakes, let it sit out for 10 minutes, and then put it in the freezer for 10 minutes. Take the cake out of the pan and put it back in the fridge wrapped in plastic wrap until it's completely cool. Or if you're eager to eat it immediately, place it on the cake stand and frost it.

Orange
Cake

Ingredients:

CAKE

1 cup olive oil
1 cup sugar
⅓ cup Just Egg
2 cups flour
1 cup freshly squeezed orange juice
Zest of 1 orange
1 Tbsp baking powder
1 tsp vanilla extract

SIMPLE SYRUP

½ cup sugar
½ cup water

WHIPPED CREAM

1 ¼ cup heavy cream
¼ cup + 1 Tbsp powdered sugar
½ tsp vanilla extract
2 drops orange food coloring

Directions:

1. Preheat the oven to 350°F. Start with the cake batter: In a medium-sized bowl, mix the oil and sugar together until smooth and grainy.
2. Add in the Just Egg, orange juice, orange zest, and vanilla extract and mix. After that, add the rest of the ingredients (the flour and baking powder) and mix until it forms a cake batter.
3. Spoon it into a prepared pan and bake for 25–30 minutes.
4. Take it out of the pan and let it cool for five minutes. Make the simple syrup on the stove. It is done when the sugar melts and the mixture simmers. With a pastry brush or spoon, pour or brush the mixture over the cake and let it soak while the cakes are still hot.
5. Combine all the ingredients for the whipped cream and mix using a handheld or stand mixer (making sure to add ingredients one by one as the mixture is mixing) until it becomes thick and spreadable; don't overmix it or it will separate. (If you want the whipped cream to be super sweet, you can add another tablespoon or two of sugar. But the cake is already sweet, so the semisweet whipped cream really balances it.)
6. Put the whipped cream on top of the cake and enjoy a nice, huge slice.

This recipe is dedicated to my great-grandmother, who would make this cake for her family every time they went over to her house; they would look forward to eating it every time. My mother said, "I would sit on the couch and smell it in the oven every time I went over to her house, and I would eat a huge slice of cake every time. There wasn't a time when this cake wasn't baking in the oven when we went to visit."

Vanilla Chocolate Swirl Cake

Ingredients:

CAKE

1 cup vegetable oil
1 cup granulated sugar
1 ½ tsp vanilla extract
¼ cup Just Egg
1 cup hot milk
1 Tbsp baking powder
2 cups all-purpose flour

CHOCOLATE SWIRL

½ cup heavy cream, hot
¼ cup milk chocolate chips

OREO FROSTING

2 sticks softened unsalted butter
3 cups confectioners' sugar
⅛ tsp salt
1 tsp vanilla extract
2 Tbsp milk
7 Oreos (crushed to powder) + extra Oreos for the in between layers

GARNISH

Homemade or store-bought brownies and cookies

Directions:

1. Preheat the oven to 350°F. Mix the oil and sugar in a medium-sized bowl until combined.
2. Add the wet ingredients group (vanilla extract, Just Egg, hot milk) to the oil and sugar and mix. Then add the dry ingredients group (baking powder and all-purpose flour) until it forms a cake batter. Pour the batter into two prepared pans (sprayed with nonstick cooking spray and lined with parchment paper).
3. Make the chocolate swirl: Combine the two ingredients, and when it is all a consistent brown color and a thick and melted chocolate consistency, swirl it into the batter with a toothpick. To do this, pour a little bit of the chocolate mixture all over the cake batter that is already in the pan and then take a toothpick to swirl the cake batter around with the chocolate.
4. Bake for 25–30 minutes, or until the toothpick comes out clean.
5. While the beautifully baked cakes cool, make the frosting: Combine the butter until perfectly smooth, then add the sugar, salt, vanilla, and milk and mix until fluffy and soft looking. Fold in the Oreos and put the mixture into a piping bag.
6. Stack the cake with frosting and crushed Oreos in between the layers. Pipe the top with the frosting, and then pile your favorite brownies and cookies on top of the cake. For the border on the bottom, break apart the brownies and cookies into pieces and arrange them in a nice pattern around the bottom layer of the cake. Now slice into it and enjoy!

Tip! To see if your cake is done, poke the center with a wooden skewer. If the skewer comes out clean, with no batter or cake crumbles sticking to it, the cake is done. If there is any batter on the stick, keep the cake in the oven for another few minutes!

Cinnamon &
Cardamom Cake

Ingredients:

CAKE

1 cup vegetable oil
1 cup granulated sugar
1 Tbsp baking powder
½ tsp ground cinnamon
¼ tsp ground cardamom
2 cups all-purpose flour
½ cup buttermilk
½ cup milk
1 tsp vanilla extract
¼ cup Just Egg

BURFI FILLING

1 cup half-and-half
¾ cup heavy cream
1 14 oz can sweetened condensed milk
½ cup sliced almonds
½ tsp ground cardamom
1 cup coconut shreds
1 Tbsp all-purpose flour

CREAM CHEESE FROSTING

1 stick softened unsalted butter
8 oz cream cheese
⅛ tsp salt
¾ tsp vanilla extract
2 cups powdered sugar
1 Tbsp milk

TOPPING

Coconut shreds

Directions:

1. Turn the oven on to 350°F and start making the cake.
2. Put the oil and sugar into a medium-sized bowl and whisk until it combines.
3. In the same bowl, whisk the wet ingredients group (buttermilk, milk, vanilla extract, and Just Egg) into the oil and sugar mixture for a couple of minutes; add the dry ingredients group (baking powder, ground cinnamon, ground cardamom, and all-purpose flour) to the wet ingredients mixture and mix until it forms a cake batter.
4. Bake for 25–30 minutes, or until the toothpick comes out clean. While it's baking, make the filling.
5. Put the half-and-half and heavy cream on the stove and bring it to a boil, which will take around 10 minutes on medium heat.
6. Then, add condensed milk and mix it in until smooth and one consistency. Once smooth, add sliced almonds, ground cardamom and coconut shreds. Keep stirring on the heat until it becomes thicker, which will take around 15 minutes, then put the hot mixture in a glass container. Be careful; the glass will be super hot! Let it cool for a little bit in the container, then put it in the fridge to fully cool and thicken.
7. Now, make the frosting: Combine the butter and cream cheese until smooth; add in the sugar and beat until it fully mixes in with the butter and cream cheese. Then, add the salt, vanilla extract, and milk until it is creamy and has no more lumps of sugar or cream cheese.
8. Once everything is cooled, assemble the cake by adding a ring of frosting on the first layer, then add the burfi filling in the middle until there is enough and it is leveled with the ring of frosting around the outer edge. Put the other cake on top and spread the frosting all over the top of the cake. After frosting, cover the top with coconut shreds to make it look like a snowball! Enjoy!

This cake is dedicated to my Indian grandmother (Dadi) because the flavors of this cake are her favorites: warm spices, nuts, and coconut! She's always had a sweet tooth and loves Indian desserts with a lot of exotic flavors. She also gave me the ingredients for the filling recipe, so I put her delicious ingredients into this wonderful recipe!

Rainbow

I want you to close your eyes and have someone read this to you. Imagine playing in the rain with your best friends. All of a sudden, the rain stops and the sun comes shining out, leaving a beautiful array of colors painting the sky. You take your measuring cup and scoop the colors into a bowl to make a rainbow dessert! It would be so cool if we could climb up and take the colors out of a rainbow. But food coloring is like a liquid rainbow, so use the perfect amount to make all these colors shine through your desserts.

Cloud Cookie with Rainbow Milkshake

Ingredients:

BANANA COOKIE DOUGH (GROUP 1)

2 sticks softened unsalted butter
1 cup granulated sugar
1 tsp vanilla extract
½ tsp banana extract
¼ cup Just Egg

BANANA COOKIE DOUGH (GROUP 2)

½ tsp baking soda
Pinch of salt
2 cups all-purpose flour

VANILLA MILKSHAKE

5 scoops vanilla ice cream
½ cup milk
1 banana
1 cup ice
Rainbow pack of food coloring

COOKIE/MILKSHAKE TOPPING

White cotton candy
Red whipped cream

Directions:

1. Preheat the oven to 350°F and line a baking tray with parchment paper.
2. Start on the cookie-dough batter by beating the butter and sugar until smooth.
3. Once smooth, add the Just Egg and the vanilla and banana extracts. Then, mix the group 2 ingredients in a separate bowl and add the group 2 mixture to the group 1 mixture until it forms a dough.
4. If it seems a little too wet, add more flour to the cookie dough and stick it in the fridge for 10–15 minutes. Once it seems like the dough has a moldable, edible soft clay consistency, then roll out the dough and cut out circles and place them on the parchment paper.
5. Bake for 10–12 minutes until the cookies turn a slight brown color on the sides. (If you overbake them, they won't be nice and chewy. Just make sure it doesn't look or feel wet or doughy.)
6. While they cool, make white cotton candy by spinning sugar using a cotton candy machine, or just use store-bought cotton candy. Once the cookies are completely cooled, put fluffs of cotton candy on top of each cookie to make it look like a cloud.
7. Now, make the milkshake by blending all the ingredients in the Vanilla Milkshake section (EXCEPT THE RAINBOW FOOD COLORING). Split the milkshake into equal parts based on how many colors you use and dye each section with one of the colors of the rainbow, starting with red, then orange, and so on. If you want the milkshake to look like the picture, you must freeze the milkshake between every layer, starting with purple and going backward in the rainbow. If you want to make your own beautiful creation, pour all the fun colors in a glass and it will make a fun rainbow swirl! (The red color is whipped cream, but if you don't want to add whipped cream, then just make the last layer red.)
8. Eat the cookies with the milkshake and enjoy!

Rainbow Explosion
Cake Pops

Ingredients:

LEMON CAKE POP (GROUP 1)

1 ¼ cups all-purpose flour
1 tsp baking powder
½ tsp salt
1 stick unsalted butter
¾ cup granulated sugar

LEMON CAKE POP (GROUP 2)

½ cup applesauce
1 ½ tsp vanilla extract
Zest of 1 medium-sized lemon
½ cup milk
2 tsp lemon juice
Food coloring

COATING AND FROSTING MIX

1 stick softened unsalted butter
4 Tbsp confectioners' sugar
Multicolored candy-coated chocolate
1–2 tsp vegetable shortening

Directions:

1. Put the oven to 350°F and get your small cake pans. (I used mini cake pans, but if you don't have those, use other pans that will help you keep the colored layers separate for baking.)
2. Start on the cake pop batter. Combine the flour, baking powder, and salt in group 1 in a small bowl and set it aside for now.
3. In a separate bowl, beat the butter and sugar until smooth and then add the group 2 ingredients (EXCEPT THE MILK AND FOOD COLORING) one by one into the mixer while it is beating the rest of the ingredients into the mixture. Make sure each ingredient is mixed in fully.
4. Switch between adding the group 1 dry ingredients and the milk (starting with the dry) to the group 2 mixture until all ingredients are in the bowl, ending with the group 1 dry ingredients.
5. Count the number of colors you have and split the batter into that many bowls. Mix a few drops of each color in their separate bowls and fully mix the color in so the batter doesn't have streaks of food coloring. Now, put the batters in their separate cake pans and bake for 15 minutes or until a toothpick comes out clean when you poke each of the individual cakes.
6. Let the cakes cool a little bit (it's ok if they're still a little warm when you start breaking them) and make the buttercream. Add the butter and sugar together and mix until fully combined. Take the cakes out of the pans and put them in separate bowls so you can add a little bit of buttercream to each color of cake. Mix the buttercream in the different bowls of cake until they come together and are fully combined with the cream. Once that is done, start assembling.
7. Take a very tiny amount of each color of cake and smush them all together in one round ball.
8. Melt a little bit of the coating chocolate and dip the cake pop sticks in the chocolate and insert them in the cake pops (this ensures that the cake will stick to the cake pop stick when you insert the cake ball on it).
9. Put the cake pops in the fridge (preferably upright, so stick them in Styrofoam or in a container with tiny slits in the top to hold the sticks) for 15–20 minutes. You want them to solidify so they don't fall apart when you dip them.
10. Separate the multicolored candy-coated chocolates in different bowls and melt each one. Add a little spoon of vegetable shortening to the different colored chocolates to thin them out if the chocolates are too thick. Once you do that, pour all the colors into one bowl and use a toothpick to swirl (not too much, though, because all the colors will blend together and turn a murky, brown color if you over mix).
11. Take the cake pops out of the fridge and dip them in the chocolate. Tap the excess chocolate off the cake pops (you can tap the top part of the stick right under the cake pop on a glass to get the excess off) and insert the sticks into Styrofoam or something that will keep them standing upright as they dry. Once dry, eat them and enjoy!

Rainbow Cake

Ingredients:

VANILLA CONFETTI CAKE

1 cup vegetable oil
1 cup granulated sugar
2 tsp vanilla extract
¼ cup Just Egg
1 cup almond milk
2 ½ cups cake flour
1 Tbsp baking powder
Sprinkles

ALMOND BUTTERCREAM

3 sticks unsalted butter
4 cups confectioners' sugar
1 ½ tsp vanilla extract
1 tsp almond extract
2 Tbsp milk
Rainbow food coloring

Directions:

1. Preheat the oven to 350°F and spray your small Bundt pans with baking spray that has flour in it.
2. Start off by whisking the vegetable oil and sugar in a large bowl.
3. Add the vanilla extract, Just Egg, and almond milk to the same large bowl.
4. Then, mix in the cake flour and baking powder until fully combined.
5. Fold in the rainbow sprinkles after the batter ingredients are mixed fully together. Pour the batter into the mini Bundt cake pans. Bake in the oven for 20 minutes or until the cakes are fully cooked. Let them cool and start on the buttercream.
6. Beat the butter and confectioners' sugar together until they form a soft and grainy texture.
7. Add the vanilla and almond extracts while the machine is still mixing. Once that is mixed in—it might take a few minutes—add the milk to make it fluffy.
8. Split the frosting into little bowls and color them with food dye. Put the colors in a piping bag, piling each color on top of another. Or line up the colors on plastic wrap and roll it up and put in the piping bag to get all the colors in a nice form.
9. Pipe the frosting on top of the cakes any way you would like and enjoy!

Tip! I learned my buttercream trick from watching videos online; you can learn a lot of tips and tricks with a little online research, so never be afraid to explore a little bit on the internet.

Rainbow
Napoleon

Ingredients:

1 small container (16 oz) heavy whipping cream
1 16 oz bottle of half-and-half
3 Tbsp cornstarch
2 Tbsp granulated sugar (may need more if it needs to be sweeter)
1 sheet puff pastry dough
Rainbow food coloring
Confectioners' sugar

This recipe is dedicated to my Armenian grandmother (Mimom). She gave me this delicious recipe, and we always cook and bake many Middle Eastern treats together. She told me that back when it wasn't possible to share recipes online, they wrote down recipes that their friends had told them about and spread them around to each other so everyone had the recipe!

Tip! You don't have to make one big pan of Napoleon; they can be made as individual pieces too! To do this, cut the dough into squares before you bake them and then just follow the recipe.

Directions:

1. First, preheat your oven to 350°F and bake your puff pastry on a sheet pan until it becomes golden brown on top, around 30 minutes (keep watching it to make sure it doesn't burn). Then, set it aside until needed.
2. While the puff pastry is baking, add the heavy whipping cream and half-and-half in a medium-sized pot and mix on medium heat. After 20 seconds, turn off the heat and set aside 1 cup of the mixture and then turn the heat back on.
3. When the heat is back on, let the mixture boil. While that is happening, take the mixture you set aside and add the cornstarch to it and mix until there are no lumps on the bottom.
4. Once the mixture in the pot starts to form bubbles on the side, add the cornstarch mixture to the pot and mix. Keep cooking the mixture until it thickens, which could take around 5 minutes or more (but make sure to keep checking on it so it doesn't burn). The longer you cook, the thicker it gets, so depending on whether you like super thick cream or a lighter cream, you'll cook it more or less.
5. Take it off the stove and put it in a bowl with the granulated sugar, then beat it with a handheld mixer.
6. Put the cream in the fridge to cool and cut your baked puff pastry in half through the middle in a horizontal form. The top will be super flaky, so poke the top lightly to press all the flakes off and put them in a bowl for later.
7. Once the cream has cooled, separate it into different bowls and color them with food dye (only a few drops in each bowl) to make the colors of the rainbow.
8. Put the cream in a nice line in rainbow order. Put the other half of the puff pastry on top.
9. Put the rest of the cream in rainbow order on top of that puff pastry. Lastly, add the flakes of the puff pastry and dust the top with powdered sugar and enjoy!

Rainbow and Gold Cupcakes

Ingredients:

RAINBOW CUPCAKE

Same recipe for the Vanilla Chocolate Swirl Cake but without the chocolate part

Rainbow food coloring

GOLDEN OREO FROSTING

1 ½ sticks softened unsalted butter

2 cups confectioners' sugar

⅛ tsp salt

1 tsp vanilla extract

8 finely crushed (to powder) Golden Oreos (plus extra for topping)

Directions:

1. Start by making the cupcakes the same way you made the cake batter for the Vanilla Chocolate Swirl Cake (without the swirl), but this time split the batter into several different bowls and color each with one color of the rainbow for each bowl.
2. After that, scoop a little bit of each color in each cupcake holder and bake for 20 minutes at 350°F. Make sure the toothpick comes out clean and the cupcakes cool all the way.
3. Now, make the frosting by beating the butter, sugar, and salt.
4. Add the vanilla extract and mix until perfectly smooth and fluffy.
5. Once smooth, fold in the crushed Oreos until they are fully mixed in. Put the frosting mixture into a piping bag.
6. Pipe the frosting on top of the cupcakes and add more crushed Golden Oreos in the middle of the swirl. Cut into these beautiful cupcakes and enjoy!

Thank you for coming along the journey of baking a cake with me and learning different tips and tricks! I hope you had fun!

Rainbow Sprinkle Star-Shaped Cookies

Ingredients:

COOKIE BASE

2 cups all-purpose flour (may need extra for rolling)
2 sticks unsalted butter, room temperature
⅔ cup granulated sugar
2 tsp vanilla extract
⅛ tsp salt
1 ½ tsp baking powder
½ cup rainbow sprinkles

VANILLA FROSTING

1 ½ sticks softened unsalted butter
1 ¼ cups granulated sugar
½ cup confectioners' sugar
½ tsp vanilla extract
⅛ tsp salt
2 Tbsp milk
More sprinkles!

Directions:

1. Start by preheating the oven to 350°F and lining your cookie tray with parchment paper.
2. Beat the butter and sugar in a medium-sized bowl for five minutes.
3. Add in the vanilla extract and salt until it combines evenly.
4. Slowly mix the flour and baking powder. Once it forms a doughy consistency, immediately mix in the rainbow sprinkles.
5. Pour the dough on a floured counter and roll out the dough. Cut them into star shapes and place them on the tray. Put the tray in the fridge for 10 minutes so the cookies hold their shape.
6. Bake for 10–12 minutes, then remove to cool. Don't overbake them so they stay nice and chewy.
7. Start on the frosting: Beat the butter and both types of sugar together until the butter and sugar turn into a soft paste texture.
8. Add vanilla extract and salt. Once it is smooth, beat in the milk until the mixture is creamy and way fluffier and lighter in color.
9. Once cooled, pipe a border of vanilla frosting around the star and add sprinkles on top. Enjoy!

Ria Lala lives in Los Angeles, California. She has always loved eating sugary sweets, so she decided to create SugaRia: a baking business with eggless treats. She began creating the recipes in this cookbook when she was thirteen years old. In the future, she hopes to invent new desserts that can be shared worldwide.

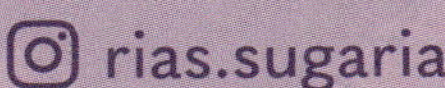